The Soul of the Artist

Spiritual Inspiration for the Christian Creative

Ramon Torres

High Bridge Books
Houston

To my parents, Frank and Yolanda Torres, who continually helped and encouraged me throughout my life.

Contents

Chapter 1

The Artist's Calling

Perhaps you're like me... Someone who grew up watching monochromatic images of Mickey and Judy (If you can't relate to those ancient two, how about Fred and Ginger? Tai and Babalonia?), expending copious amounts of energy entertaining Depression era masses. In spite of the surmounting antiquity of it all, you were thrilled to the point where you were brought to your feet exclaiming, "I can do that!"

So consumed in your enthusiasm, every chance to show off what you could do was seized with a generous amount of gusto. In which case, there were choirs and high school productions as well as (maybe) some barnyard performances. On top of all that, there were classes in voice, dance, and maybe an instrument here or there with theatrical (drama) lessons thrown in the mix.

Or, perhaps at an early age, just like the young Mozart, you were recognized to possess an innate talent. A talent that was encouraged and developed in every childhood class your parents could afford. Then, there were the recitals, the competitions, or even a pageant or two. However humble the beginnings, you knew you just had to get out there and do what you knew you were born to do.

Humble Beginnings

On a more personal note... There are many significant images that crowd my memory. The earliest is of me standing with some classmates at some school function. I waved, a lady laughed, and I entirely enjoyed the attention. She may not have been reacting to what I was doing, but the whole, momentary experience was enough for me to decide to do such things more often.

Pure and simple... singing comes very naturally to me. My mother used to say that I sang before I talked. Unlike Mozart, I wasn't seen as any child prodigy. The majority of my "early lessons" came from exposure to the black and white musicals that played continually on the local networks.

One of my all-time favorites was Jimmy Cagney's *Yankee Doodle Dandy*. At the end of the film, there's a scene where Jimmy dances/taps down an interior White House staircase. Just as all children imitate something they've seen, I wanted to do that, too. One day, during a shopping trip to a neighborhood department store, I found my chance to try my Terpsichore prowess. Truth was, then (and today), I had none. That didn't stop me from trying.

During my early "formative" years, I got into the dangerous habit of comparisons. If I was not "as good as so and so," then I couldn't have been any good (I would say to myself). And I was fairly convinced of this bit of news.

So I would down play my talent. "Anybody can sing," I'd say. After all, around holiday time, everybody would join around the piano and sing carols. Or at other occasions, people would accent a good time by belting out a few tunes. I would think, "What's the big deal?" And yet, deep down, it was a big deal to me. I felt there was something "different" about my talent.

A good majority of my friends could carry a tune and, for the most part, they were content to sing just for the heck of it. But, for me, I found that I just wasn't content to just vocalize. As I grew older, I felt compelled to broaden my range. With each type of music (whether it was Classical, Jazz, Folk, Rock, or the Blues), I felt challenged to "master" whatever style there was to the best of my ability. The very experience of filling my lungs with air to push out each note and cadence was a total thrill.

Then, there was the fact that, throughout my life, people wouldn't fail to compliment me on my voice. Take for instance the time when I was in the Navy, stationed La Madalena, Italy. One afternoon, I dropped in to see my friend, Maria. It just so happened that some of her relatives, from a nearby town, were there for a visit. Welcoming me in, she introduced me and, almost immediately plopped a guitar in my hands and ordered me to sing. Upon finishing my song, the whole group broke into applause. Her cousin pumped my hand enthusiastically declaring, "Bellisima!"

Whenever teenage Ramon brought up the desire to perform professionally, most of the adults I knew said show business was not a stable or reliable type of employment. On top of it all, the old platitude that "anybody could sing" (and, therefore, it was nothing special) kept echoing within the walls of my mind. Truth be told, it was a deep fear to break out on my own, to pursue a professional career. Therefore, I felt (to feel "safe") I had to keep my light beneath the proverbial bushel.

For a good thirty years, my life was filled with countless choirs and talent shows, and yet I still felt very frustrated. One big problem that kept rearing its ugly head was that singing brought tremendous joy to me, and I couldn't hide it. If music was on in the office, I wouldn't think twice about joining in. As in all situations, there were those who didn't share my enthusiasm for such things. On more than one occasion, I was told that singing was not appropriate for the professional working space. So, at the ripe young age of 56, I decided to quit my safe job and brave it on that final frontier of *Show Biz!*

From the specific to the general

For all of my fellow Christian performers who share my artistic proclivities, what choices do we have? To my way of thinking, the alternatives are few. We have to align ourselves to a business that allows us to utilize these God-given gifts. There are just too few options of venues out there that will allow us to sing, dance, act, and what have you.

It is indeed a daunting and yet necessary step for all of us to make. Becoming "stars" is not a necessary or feasible dream. We just need the work. There are hundreds of professional theater companies (not necessarily

Community Theaters) where fame may elude us, but they offer work nonetheless.

Aside from the diverse and possible employment opportunities, (if you're anything like me) and you've grown up being told that Show Biz is no kind of career for somebody who believes in God, there's a major inner struggle. Adding more and more insult to the pain, the church and the Arts, in general, have not gotten along for centuries.

Church history and the arts

Tertullian, one of the Early Church Fathers, wrote a piece called, *De Spectaculis*. This was a document that dealt with morality of theater attendance for Christians. After all, the profane theatrical content, even then, was not conducive to the morals of any man. The same was true for the dramatic fare of the subsequent centuries, not to mention the attitude towards the participants. Actors were seen as unstable, untrustworthy, loosely moral beings who were not fit to be around.

Artists didn't fair too much better than the actors. While the magnificent works of Michelangelo and Leonardo da Vinci graced the walls of the early churches, their work came under suspicion. Ecclesiastical authorities decided that the artwork would promote and endorse idolatry. Therefore, they would discourage the use of art in places of worship.

A secondary effect of this crackdown was that many artists (painters, "pencillers," and sculptors) found themselves constrained in the sort of work they could produce. In other words, the church hierarchy would not allow them to paint anything that was not "Christian" or Biblically inspired.

Modern church attitudes toward artists

Unfortunately, Christian attitudes toward the arts have not changed. In these modern times, there is still a suspicion toward anything that does not fall within the parameters of what is considered Christian. While I don't want to over-generalize the point, some Christians still need a very explicit spiritual message. They feel that there needs to be a specific Christ-figure, pastor, saint, or church-goer who spouts Scripture or perhaps someone who has "seen the light" at the end of the opus. This point was keenly illustrated to me when I read of a woman who didn't see a Christian message in the 2005 release of C.S. Lewis' *The Lion, the Witch, and the Wardrobe.*

This is what happened: Prior to the release of the ground breaking film, *Charisma* magazine wrote an article about it. As is the custom, a few issues later, readers sent letters in response to it. There were a few in praise of it, but this one lady wrote that she didn't see a Christian message in it. Much to my surprise, she failed to equate Aslan's substitutionary death for his friends with Christ's work on the cross. It was more than apparent that the allusion escaped her.

What to do?

So, what are we Christian performers to do? While there are more and more churches that use drama, dance, and more creative music, there really aren't many places that can afford to sustain professional art troupes. Besides, there really wouldn't be enough work to keep the job satisfying, challenging, and creative. One would only be working Sundays and holidays. There are a few Christian theater companies, but even they are insufficient to keep an actor alive and kicking. That means *we have to* brave the cold, cruel world of Show Business.

Of course, there are those who have already discovered this fact. Those staunch survivors of a very insecure lifestyle that guarantees neither hope nor creative satisfaction. Many of us have braved the routine of cold, relentless open auditions and the endless uncertain amounts of down-time. In spite of all the negative aspects, it can be said that we don't know any better, and we should be considered candidates for a rubber room, but we continue because… we don't know any better.

For those of us who have jobs that "pay the bills," we do what we can to keep going and succeed. And yet, there's more than just surviving, more than just enduring for the long haul. Our very hearts and souls have to be fed and maintained in order for us to mature spiritually and hold on to our sanity.

The church is indeed in need of Christian professional artists (singers, dancers, actors, etc.), yet it is especially true for the "business"—for all of us who take Christ's admonition at the end of the Gospel of Matthew seriously—that is, to go out into all the world and make disciples, to teach them "what I have taught you."

We are more than aware that we are to be the *salt* (preservative, the seasoning which brings out the God-flavors of this earth). We are also the *light* that illuminates God's love for all to see. That "world" of Show Business especially needs our salt and light. We are the soldiers of the Cross to whom God has entrusted the Good News of His saving grace.

Just as that light won't be seen hidden under some basket, we, the bearers of the light, won't be seen within the confines of a church's walls. The instructions were to "go out" to the nations of the world. It is a pleasure to fellowship with other Christian artists in our local congregations but, as the Lord pointed out, it is not the healthy that need a doctor.

For all of us who feel our "spiritual" legs are weak beneath us, we have the blatant assurance that He is with us always. He has not sent us out alone. His "Comforter," His Holy Spirit, is standing right next to us, guiding us into all truth. Therefore, we shouldn't feel afraid. We need to get out there because the harvest is plentiful, but the laborers are few.

You are qualified by God

All of us are born having to "adapt" to this world. Just about each day could be filled with challenges (some major, some minor) that force us to learn some lessons of survival.

One of my earliest childhood memories was telling my older sister at the dinner table that I was going to cover myself in white soap. When she asked why, I told her that it was because I didn't want to look different than the other kids in my kindergarten class. It didn't happen, but it's apparent that I could see how my brown skin singled me out. Years went by, and my friends would tease me, not only because of my dark complexion, but because of my coarse, "Brillo" like hair, my height, and my weight. Oh sure, I learned how to dish it back in style, but I really didn't want to be singled out for whatever reason. On the surface, I could laugh it off, and yet, deep down, nobody wants to be on "the outside." With all of these elements in play, my self-image was not a very good one.

It would be nice and maybe easy to believe that I would just grow out of my low self-esteem, but the thoughts and feelings had a hold on my psyche. During 1983, while in my thirties, I took part in a church internship in Columbus, Ohio. It was an experience shared with one other guy (Dave) and two ladies (Linda and Barbara). For almost a full year, we fulfilled various and sundry Sunday tasks in the church body, including hospital visitation, church set up, and worship-leading. There were also those times when we just hung out together.

On one of those occasions, I sat in Dave's living room, watching television with him and his family. Situated in a spot no one could miss was a picture of Dave in a basketball uniform. There he was in all of his six-foot-tall, athletic, slim glory, being acknowledged as the team's Most Valuable Player. It's not that I wanted to be great at any sport, but I still felt "dwarfed" by this picture. In some ways, it was hard just to be around it because I knew it could never happen to me. So, I sat there that night and glanced at the photo and said to myself, "I could never do that." (And I knew that I didn't mean posing in a basketball uniform.) The minute I thought that, a very distinct, deliberate voice asked, "Why not?"

Along with feeling that didn't belong anywhere in particular, I really didn't feel secure in who I was. I always had a self-deprecating wise crack, ready at a moment's notice. For example, I heard that a person who wanted to go into Christian service would have to receive a "call" into ministry. For me, with my poor self-image, I knew I wasn't going to get a call but rather a postcard with postage due. At that moment in Dave's living room, I just was not accustomed to thinking too positively about myself. When I heard the question, I knew it wasn't coming from me, and it shook me to the core. I knew that the Lord was telling me that my thinking was going to have to change, which didn't happen overnight. Nevertheless, this was a profound moment in my life.

Very few people on this planet escape struggling with inner feelings of inadequacy. But I have learned that God doesn't want us to carry any unnecessary burdens with us. He has ways of training his soldiers… if we let Him.

Chapter 2

The Artist's Identity

So, we are artists—dancers, singers, actors, writers, etc.—and as far as I'm concerned, the creative bent is the highest calling in life. It totally outranks that of doctors, politicians, truck drivers, scientists, cops, and especially lawyers. But, then again, I am *extremely* biased.

Acting, when done right, can be a healing art form. The same goes for music. When King Saul (of Old Testament fame) was beset by all sorts of problems and worries, it was only David's playing that soothed his mangled nerves. Music's comforting power has been recognized throughout the centuries. In the 17th century, William Congreve wrote, "Music hath charms to sooth the savage breast." Another English poet wrote, "If music be the food of life, play on."

We hypersensitive, creative people have "a lot of heart." Often, it is us who hold up the mirror to the rest of the world in order for them to recognize the truth.

Through his writings, Charles Dickens magnified the plight of the poor. Paul Robeson trained to be a lawyer, but it was his splendid singing that gave voice to the condition of the black man in America. Scads and scads of artists such as Martin Sheen and Harry Belafonte have not given a second thought to the consequences of putting aside their own comforts to shed light on many of the problems that plague us human beings.

Unfortunately, to those in the "outside world," we are seen as very temperamental in nature, mercurial in mood and our commitments. Here are some other adjectives that follow us: free-spirited, fickle, flakey, immature, quirky, and unreliable. Perhaps the least negative of them all would be "dreamers." Yet, the connotation, "dreamer," implies that our feet aren't firmly tethered to this world and that we are of no earthly good. Of course, one of our possible lines of justification is the "I'm rubber, you're glue" defense, which could be followed by the "Sez you!" school of apologetics.

Plainly spoken, there is a modicum of truth to just about everything said about us. We either develop a thick skin to all the verbal barbs directed toward us, or we become overly sensitive and defensive, which is not good. The prickly, easily offended artist is very hard to be around. People start walking on the proverbial egg shells when they're around such folks. We all have to come to a true and scathingly honest assessment of who we really are, a state that only be arrived at by learning to love ourselves.

Let's face it. We're not born knowing who we truly are and how to love ourselves. The majority of us grow up becoming a crazy quilt of our parents' ambitions, moral beliefs, and insecurities. After all, that's how they started out. It's a cyclical motion that goes on from generation to generation. Generally, your parents didn't know what it is to love themselves because their predecessors didn't know how. Therefore, they would not know of the importance of passing down this information. Blessed are they who come to this life giving knowledge, but they'd be in a rather small minority. Only God can teach us how to love.

We are God's masterpiece

Who Am I This Time? is a short story by Kurt Vonnegut. His main character, Harry Nash, is an extremely shy hardware store worker, who finds it excruciatingly hard to relate to other people. Like so many shy people, he prefers to keep his own company. Oddly enough, Harry's saving grace is the stage. He finds his tongue (as well as his emotions) through the words of theater's premier writers. Harry comes alive when he's given the chance to play Stanley Kowalsky in Tennessee Williams' *A Street Named Desire*.

This may be a somewhat extreme example, but it's all too true for all artists, to a degree. The source of their identity, who they are, is their talent. "I'm a dancer." "I'm a writer." So on and so on and so on. The plain fact of the matter is that this is true of all people. Many lives are caught up in their ambitions and goals. Doctors, lawyers, teachers, and judges all fill up with pride being who they are. The big problem is that such aspirations are not enough to build a life upon.

Because there is no instruction booklet on how to live, we all fill ourselves with ideas and images of what we'd like to be (how we'd like to be perceived). A good many of our ideas and notions come from our families, for they have the earliest impact on what makes us who we are. Then, there's the media. Just as comedians, such as the Marx Brothers and Lou Costello, made an indelible impression on my psyche, children through the ages will be influenced by the likes of Michael Jackson and Lady Gaga.

One major (very injurious) aspect of media incitement is the world's obsession with beauty. Ah yes! It's as if it were yesterday. Little Ramon (younger, at least) would be sitting in front of the television set, and this very attractive blonde girl would burst upon the screen. She'd be running along the beach, giggling and laughing, as she's being playfully chased by some guys. Or, there she was, driving around in a convertible with the top down with the wind cascading through those beautiful locks of hers, looking as if she didn't have a care in the world. "If I have only one life, let me live it as a blonde!" was her life affirming declaration (Undoubtedly, inspired by Patrick Henry's famous quote, "Give me liberty or give me death."). Any way you look at it, this was a very stimulating, motivating view.

Needless to say, I wanted that life! Not that I wanted to be chased by a bunch of guys, but I was more than open to believe that "Blondes have more fun!" I wanted that fun! Who wouldn't? The whole intent of the ad was to make us feel lousy about our lives so we'd go out and buy their product. The background, subliminal message was that if we use this hair dye, our lives would be vastly improved.

Being caught up with outward beauty is, indeed, not a modern world concept. Women in Cleopatra's day knew how to bedeck themselves in captivating and beguiling ways. In the 18th century, corsets were invented to give women that "ideal, smaller waist." Some women went as far as to have ribs removed to gain this all important concept of perfection. Both sexes (yes, some men wore corsets too) are more than willing to do anything to adhere to what the world considers beautiful. Sadly enough, you can be the "Fairest in the Land" (or, the most handsome) and just not see it in yourself because of your lack of love for who you really are.

Love yourself

In order to know what it is to truly love yourself, you must first learn what it is to love God. When you've made that commitment to seek after God, it is the first step in a life-altering, fulfilling journey. Like anything important in life, it's an initial task that is in no way easy to attain. You will struggle with old ways of thinking: ideas, concepts, and attitudes you've believed to be true your whole life.

Here is one really big "fer instance." During a particular "overnight" stop in my journey (of which there were many), I found that I had to learn that God really did love me. Oh sure, I knew what my pastors had told me. Heck! I had a Sunday School hymn to reassure me of the fact: "Jesus loves me this I know..." For all intents and purposes, I could shout it from the housetops that He did, and yet, deep down, I really wasn't sure. Plain truth, I was scared. Scared that He'd have me do something I really didn't want to do like send me to be a missionary in some far off place, but then I read a passage in the Living Bible that lifted a burden off my spirit:

> We need have no fear of someone who loves us perfectly; his perfect love for us eliminates all dread of what he might do to us. If we are afraid, it is for fear of what he might do to us and shows us that we are not fully convinced that He really loves us. (1 John 4:18)

After reading that, I was *more than convicted* by God's Holy Spirit that I had to confess my unbelief because it was only holding me back from fully experiencing all that God had for me. This revelation made a total difference in my outlook on everything I did. There are still times when I have to be reminded of this fact, for it's all part of the building of my faith.

The purifying process

Throughout the Bible, fire is used a symbol of God. The first epistle of Peter alludes to the purifying effects fire has on gold. Moses stood before the burning bush, making the area holy and sanctified. So it is with us. When we draw closer to God, more of who we are is exposed in His Holy light. Because sin can't survive in God's presence, His magnificent light will burn away areas of sin in our lives, areas that prevent us from getting closer to Him. In His bright and purifying fire, we will see these layers as lies because they are not of Him. Only when we concede and confess it all as sin can we truly relax in His love.

It's a pruning and cropping process. The fifteenth chapter of John's Gospel tells us that Christ is the true vine, and we are the branches. It is the vine of the grape plant that is rooted into the ground. Through these roots, the fruit receives the water, minerals, and nutrients it needs to sustain its life. In other words, the Lord is the source of who we are. He made us; therefore, detached from Him, we only receive a sham of a life.

My life has been pretty long, and I've learned that one should not chase after the shallow aspects of it all. Perhaps there's that certain look you feel you have to achieve before you'll consider yourself complete. That will cause you to short-change yourself. These belief systems are primarily facades to shut out others from finding out we aren't as together as we'd like them to believe. It's all a cover up because we really don't want to admit to ourselves how we truly hurt down deep.

Chapter 3

The Artist's Character

Adrian Monk (played by Tony Shaloub on the hit TV show, *Monk*) had this little saying when he defended his super-special detective abilities: "It's a blessing, and it's a curse." This is how I feel about the artistic temperament. Being creatively driven can be an overwhelming, satisfying way to live, but it can also be something of a devastating burden.

Much joy can be derived from bringing your ideas to life, but then you have to put up with a nagging, insatiable inner life of fears and doubts that can assail and undermine your sense of security. Maybe what we're doing isn't good enough. Or, maybe people won't like and appreciate what we're doing. Hundreds of similar, internal, and infernal thoughts can corrode our joy. It's especially painful because our creativity and talent is wrapped up in what makes us who we are.

Then, there are the external pressures. Despite the fact you've spent your multitudinous years with your family, they really don't understand who we are most of the time. Too many family reunions of mine were spent staring into stucco faces, trying to share the things closest to my heart.

Not only are they not interested, their understanding of the arts, in general, *leaves* much to be desired. It's much akin to the painter's frustration when their kin's art preference is dogs playing poker on black velvet. The worst part comes when our personal authoritative types (parents, aunts, uncles, etc.) insist on our finding "real work."

For us performers (actors, dancers, musicians, singers, etc.), we're in an unstable business. Work can be more than fleeting. It can be near non-existent. When and if we get gigs, they are too few and far between. The instability of our chosen professions only adds to an already fragile sense of security. Frustration mounts up because we feel cheated that we can't use our talents as we would like. The very nature of the business doesn't allow us to earn the living we'd like.

Unfortunately, our frustration doesn't start with our talent. The plain truth of the matter is that very few of us overcome the fallout of the emotional maelstrom known as adolescence. You can be the most beautiful person in the world and still not be satisfied with the way you look. Your nose may be too big or too small. Your boobs or biceps may not be as big as you'd like. In this world of changeable parts, such as our facial and body aspects, these things can be *fixed*. The trouble is that it's not our "disdainful anatomical features" that are the problems. Rather, it's our attitude towards our whole being. We have to learn what it is to truly love and *accept* everything about us.

As previously mentioned, growing up, I didn't like my height, skin color, or my hair. Put all of these characteristics together, and they spell, "different." Nobody likes to feel like they're on the outside and don't belong. The longer we feel at odds about ourselves, the shakier our emotional foundations will be. It is only through drawing closer to God that we can gain the total sense of acceptance we need.

He replaces the concept of love that we have believed for the majority of our lives to be "the one and only way" things should be. His kinda love is far better than anything we can come up with. It is an all-encompassing love that can fill our hearts to overflowing. We no longer see ourselves as we think we should be (those worldly concepts of beauty) or want to be. His love for who we really are can radiate through every portion of who we are.

This all-saturating love also allows us to see others as God wants us to, not as competition or threats, but as equals and as His fellow children. When this happens, we want to treat these people with the same love and respect we want to be shown.

All of this isn't some high falutin', pie in the sky, "touchy feely" sort of reaction. As long as we allow God to do what He wants with us, we will succeed. The bottom line is that the more we are focused on our shortcomings, our failings, and our needs, the less good we are to ourselves and those around us.

With this new sense of love in our lives comes a deeper respect and reverence for our bodies. We begin to see it as being "fearfully and wonderfully made" (Psa. 139:14, KJV), not just some conglomeration of changeable parts.

Weighing In

"The camera adds ten pounds." Whatever the cause for this optical phenomena, it carries with it a great concern for those who are gainfully employed in front of a camera. These performers feel compelled to adopt stringent dietary and exercise regimens to lose any "excess" weight.

One big problem is that fear has a tendency to take over, causing them to go to extremes. Unfortunately, other health problems can occur due to these strict behaviors. There needs to be a healthy balance. When we allow God to take away our fears about anything, He will replace them with His view of what we should be.

Harmony with God

Have you ever been in a working situation where you were scared about those who worked with you? For example, have you ever been in a musical and felt that another cast member was a better singer than you? Perhaps you felt their part was supposed to be yours?

The green-eyed monster can consume your life, especially if you feel cheated. Of course, things can get pretty lonely if the monster doesn't bring his good friend and companion, insecurity. Every time somebody makes a comment about you (however innocent it may be intended), and it is then received with anything less than gracious words, you can be in trouble. Anger, bitterness, and resentment (even in small doses) can hurt all of us who succumb to jealousy.

Being human, we are all susceptible to the poison of envy. We all have a tendency to engage in bouts of comparing ourselves, our talents, and our abilities with others. Such thinking can and will reinforce self-doubts if we start to feel that others' talents are better than ours. These fears can only lead to deeper self-absorption and alienation.

Another source of professional jealousy is a driving sense of perfection. Some of us have had instructors who demanded perfection from us. To add to this, we may have nurtured the attitude, deep down, that we just weren't good enough. In spite of how much we've practiced, we still found the "high bar of perfection" we have set for ourselves to be elusive. Whenever mistakes occur, we can be a little less than merciful toward ourselves.

Perfectionism, to me, is an unattainable fallacy. Fighting to achieve that perfect standard can be very dangerous, for it inhibits performances and stifles creativity. My experience as an actor has convinced me that there's no such thing as a perfect show. In some musical number, I could be following the choreography as I had done dozens of time before, but then one of my cast mates becomes momentarily distracted and forgets what we've rehearsed. A few toes are stepped on and a few elbows rubbed the wrong way, and we know it's wrong.

All you can do in those situations is keep going and not gripe about it afterwards. All artists should strive for excellence in their craft and not that supposed sense of perfection that you'll never achieve. You have to love yourself and get off your own back! Mistakes happen!

Any ties of jealousy have to be broken by prayer. Whenever you feel that green-eyed monster rearing its ugly head, we all have to seek after God and His forgiveness. The jealously and envy has to be recognized as sin and not justified away as some inalienable right. It's not going to be easy, especially when we feel we've been wronged. Beseeching the Lord for his peace could require more than one attempt. We all have to lay down our sense of what is "right," especially during those times of pain.

Love and peace go together. As I heard ol' Blue eyes, Frank Sinatra, once croon, one really can't have "one without the other." When you come to truly love yourself, peace will undoubtedly take up residence in your heart.

> And God's peace [be yours, that tranquil state of a soul assured of its salvation through Christ, and so fearing nothing from God and content with its earthly lot of whatever sort that is, that peace] which transcends all understanding, shall garrison and mount guard over your hearts and minds in Christ Jesus. (Phil. 4:7, Amplified)

The first time I experienced this kind of peace, my mind (in total Sixty's parlance) was totally blown. I learned that verse from Philippians was not just some nice words written centuries ago. The more time we spend in God's presence, the more we feel His incomprehensible peace.

When and if those times occur, when the ugly, green-eyed monster reels his all-encompassing nasty little head, you run (don't walk) to the throne of God. Get there as quickly as you can before it has a chance to fill your head and your bed with anguished, sleepless nights. You should pray a prayer like this:

Dear Lord Father, you have given me everything I need in my life. Thank you for my life, my days, and my talents. Please forgive me for every unkind thought and word within me. Such things can only poison my thinking and keep me from loving others as you want me to. Please have your way with me and my whole life. Fill me with your incomprehensible love and peace for only you are the author of my life.

Gleefully we roll along?

There's that age-old adage that states, "Patience is a virtue." This quality can lead to long lives. In our current, instant, microwave, fifteen-minutes-of-fame society, patience is a necessary modern characteristic.

Now, this may sound like a total and absolute digression from what I've been writing about, but I must say that I do not like the TV show, *Glee*. The biggest thing I hate about it is that they really don't demonstrate the reality of the learning process. Nobody is born knowing lyrics to songs, but they all start singing as if their songs come out of mid-air. Of course, Hollywood musicals have done this for years, but I can't help but feel cheated when these kids (and faculty) break out into well-choreographed routines. At least the show, *Fame*, gave a slight bit of pretense that some rehearsals were in progress.

The reality of the artist's life is that we are thrust into seclusion in order to hone our respective crafts. There is a monumental sense of achievement when we've worked at something and brought it to fruition. Nothing good ever comes easy. Diamonds undergo thousands of pounds of compression, not to mention a lot of time. So it is with us as new creatures in Christ.

"The work God has begun in us" doesn't happen overnight (Phil. 1:6). Therefore, he has to instill in us His patience—if we let Him. This virtue that the old adage spells out was usually a platitude parents would use with antsy kids. It's supposed to be something that we have to work at, but God's kind of patience is a whole lot better. Love plus peace equals patience.

Another glorified couple

In the minds of most people, goodness and kindness are essentially synonymous. If someone is kind, it stands to reason they do "good" things. That is, the acts they perform are of some benefit to others. A person who helps the proverbial old lady to cross the street comes to her aid in a time of distress. The same goes for the person who comes to rescue of another stranded on the side of the road. Both of these helpers would be perceived as *good*.

In fact, the human race is full of acts considered good deeds toward their fellow man. Atheists feel there is no need for God or religion. They contend that we only have to do "good things." Problem is, how do we measure what is good? Whose standards do we go by?

Just about everybody would agree that someone giving money to another human being down on their luck is an honorable and beneficial act. And yet, (in my mind) if the deed is done out of sense of obligation—not from willingness—it is somewhat tainted. A majority of people really don't like doing things because they have to. Acts done out of the freedom of the will do not breed contempt and resentment.

Submitting ourselves to God's way guarantees that we will be imbued with His love. Those around us become a priority. As we draw closer to Him, He clears out the hurt emotions and pain we've accumulated over our lifetimes. They are the fears and justifications that block us from true acts of goodness and kindness.

Letting go

The arts world can be a dog-eat-dog, dog-bites-man place that can be very stressful, and that is putting it mildly. We artists can be thin-skinned people, bristling at just about every nasty look and comment as I brought up earlier in these pages (and most definitely will again much later). These slights don't even have to be of an ill-tempered nature. A statement could be well-intended as a constructive, well-meaning criticism. But we only see it as an assault on our peace. Those people are seen as the enemy, not to be trusted or forgiven. All of this can be seen as right and justified, but here's where we get into trouble.

Unforgiveness is a very natural, human part of life. When we've been wronged, it's very easy to harbor ill will toward others. The problem is that unforgiveness has a way of festering in our souls. It's like a cancer that can eat away at our minds, emotions, and bodies. It can color every part of our thinking with negativity, making us very hard to be around. There have been countless medical studies that report on the devastating effects of pent up bitterness. Hypertension, due to this bitterness, can easily raise one's blood pressure and wreak havoc on their hearts.

The only remedy to the sin of unforgiveness is to forgive. It's a supernatural type of forgiveness that can only come from God. This is something that doesn't come easily or naturally. We humans have a tendency to be very stubborn when it comes to feeling justified in our unforgiveness, but with the Holy Spirit's help, it is more than possible.

Good News!

Did you know that praising God can make you beautiful? This is especially important news to those of us in the performing arts where image is just about *everything*. Yes! It's true! I've seen it with my own eyes on the faces of the young and old. Their eyes have brightened as if there were spotlights behind them. The entire countenance just appears to glow with an iridescence that is remarkable. When it's seen, it's almost impossible to look away. The explanation for this phenomenon is relatively simple. When we praise God, having become ushered into His presence, His holiness can't help but rub off on us through

His close proximity to us. One great scriptural example of this phenomenon can be seen in Matthew 17:2.

Jesus had taken Peter, James, and John high up into the mountains. Immediately, His face shone as bright as the sun. These disciples soon found they were in the Father's presence when they heard the words, "This is my Son with whom I am well pleased."

Problem is, when we harbor a sin like unforgiveness in our hearts, the light in our eyes is extinguished. Jesus said, "Your eye is the lamp of your body; when your eye is sound and fulfilling its office, your whole body is full of light" (Luke 11:34). The facial muscles around the eyes become tight with tension. This can makes us look older than we are.

Unfortunately, sin has a way of robbing us of our confidence, destroying our self-esteem. When we don't like who we are, we have a tendency to only see the negative aspects of our lives. Even when we manage to suppress (press them down deep into our psyches) the things we don't like, they're still there despite the fact we don't want to admit it. The internal struggle only adds a weight of guilt to our appearance. The Bible says, "Just as water mirrors your face your face mirrors your heart" (Prov. 27:19, The Message).

A modern representation of this change is Karla Faye Tucker. Karla was a drug addicted, party girl, who was convicted and condemned to death for the ax murder of two people. By the age of 8, she was smoking. Come 14, she was already into drugs and prostitution. Her mug shot showed a cold, blank, and lifeless stare that covered her entire face. It was a picture that couldn't illicit an ounce of sympathy from me.

While in prison, Karla Faye had an encounter with the one, true, almighty God. Her entire countenance changed. The girl was radiant; more than beautiful! She was incandescent! It was all too hard to believe and hard to turn away from. The mug shot of Karla did not depict the same woman of the subsequent photographs and film clips. Karla had undoubtedly come face-to-face with her sinful life and forgiven the people who had introduced her to it all. So must all of us who desire to thrive in God's freedom.

Being Complete

Jesus said, "Be ye perfect even as your father, which is in heaven is perfect" (Matt. 5:48, KJV). Talk about pressure! Not only do I have to make sure I didn't call my brother "raca" (which means, *idiot*), I also have to make sure that I am reconciled to him if I have "aught" (anger) against him. Then, if I were to look at a woman with lust in my heart, I would be guilty of adultery. This is an awful lot to contend with considering I want to be right with God. But, being perfect?

Believe me, I have tried, but I have missed the mark with just about every effort and on almost every occasion. It was undeniably a heavy load to carry. Or, so I thought during my formative years as Christian.

Much later on, I learned that the verse actually means that we are to be in "complete maturity of godliness in mind and character, having reached the proper heights of virtue and integrity" (Matt. 5:48, Amplified). Oy! What a tremendous load off my back! It meant that I didn't have to follow this long list of "dos and don'ts." The effort was no longer solely on my shoulders in my quest to be more like Him… in order to be "perfect."

Whenever I'd see *self-control* listed among the fruit of the Holy Spirit, it never really stood out to me; it didn't seem all that special if you know what I mean. Hey! You can't beat things like love, joy, and peace. Everybody can use a whole lot of these things. We really can't live without them. But, self-control?

For all intents and purposes, I really can't say that my life was ever really out of control. Drugs and illicit sex were never an issue. I've never really cared for the use or abuse of four letter epithets. Maybe (and this is a big maybe) I'd lose my temper about twice a year. So, I thought I had myself pretty much under *control.* Yet, as I grew in my relationship with God, I began to see a lot of subtle differences.

Plain fact of the matter is that anything of God (attributed to and given by Him) can't compare to anything we humans can come up with. It's like what Christ had said about the peace coming from Him. His sort of peace had nothing to do with what the world could conceive of or manufacture. This peace wouldn't come in a bottle nor through any political leader (John 14:27).

God's *self-control* can be seen as a supernatural sense of maturity that can affect us in multiple ways. One of the biggest, subtle changes I discovered in myself was my feeling about cursing. Even from a young age, I didn't care much for the "common vernacular." If my parents got angry, a slew of four letter words didn't come out of them. It was just not an acceptable form of communication in our household. The words were more than familiar to me. I just didn't like them.

Then, a shock was delivered while in Navy boot camp because the language was all pervasive. The guys would use the words as nouns, adjectives, and verbs—ways I had never heard before. Sometimes, I found it all to be a bit "creative." With all the cursing going on around me, I could have been very tempted to join in because it was the dominant way of the guys expressing themselves. Boot camp was more than 20 years ago, but when I'm hanging around with my fellow actors, the same type of talk can be heard.

Despite that many of my friends use the language, I find it very uncomfortable. Whenever I hear them use these words, I get this twinge of sadness inside. It hurts because these are not words of love. This is especially true when I hear them carelessly speak about other people. They don't even have to know those they are talking about. These words are a way to demean and tear down. Calling someone names is a way of saying that they aren't worth knowing. They may be a child of God, but you make it clear with those words that they have no value to you or anyone else. All over the world, laws are being enforced concerning "hate speech." If these words in the common vernacular, aren't in that category, they well should be because they certainly ain't "love speech."

Growing up like any adolescent boy, I loved action films; sometimes, the gorier, the better. When I'd see the army of good guys beat the snot out of the bad guys, the adrenaline started pumping and yells of "Get 'em!" came out of me. Yet, when I got closer to the Lord, I found it very hard to not cringe and turn away. Whenever I'd see the human body being abused for the sake of entertainment, I'd feel sick to my stomach. Today, it is very common to see bodies (and body parts) flying all over the screen. To me, this indicates a severe lack of respect for God's last and greatest creation.

As you allow the Holy Spirit to transform you, you'll find that you don't laugh at the same things you once did. More and more, as we mature, the childish, sophomoric fare portrayed in a good majority of today's TV shows and movies will become offensive.

When I was young in the church, such things were said to be avoided because they were not "Christian." It was a deliberate, conscious effort on my part to steer clear of them. Yet, the neat thing was that I found that this sense developed into an "inner radar." My heart was now attracted to fare of a definite better quality. It really didn't matter if it carried the label of "Christian."

When I see a movie such as *The Fighter*, I could be easily offended by the profanity, yet it was so skillfully integrated into the character that it was hard to turn away. These people were representative of God's creation in pain. Too much of today's entertainment abuses the "popular" four letter words to the point where it just becomes boring.

Increasing our talents

Back when I was a kid, I thought Marvel comics were the best in the world (still do). The characters just seemed to be more "human" than say, Superman and Batman of the DC ilk.

While there's no way for my memory to come up with the exact issue, I can't forget one particular installment of the *Fantastic Four*. Reed Richards, the super intelligent leader of the group, had developed this machine that augmented their powers. If memory serves me correctly, Ben Grimm's super strength became stronger and Johnny Storm's flame was increased to become nova hot. Prior to this, Sue Storm (Invisible Woman) was relegated to just turning invisible. Oh sure, she could get away without being seen, but when it came to fighting the villains, about all she could do was trip the guy or sucker punch him — when he wasn't looking, of course. But now, with her powers, she could form a force shield as well as throw invisible force bombs. Reed's stretching ability also went beyond his previous limits.

The Lord will also develop and extend our artistic abilities. Just as in the Parable of the Talents (Matt. 25:15-29), ours can increase. He doesn't use a machine, but it is done supernaturally. During the maturation process, you will find you are able to accomplish things you weren't able to do in the early years of your talent.

As a singer, your interest in music can expand; you'll get a deeper understanding and appreciation of music. Your voice may develop a deeper and stronger resonance.

Musicians can develop more of an appreciation for sound and how it relates to their instrument(s).

Dancers will gain strength with a better recognition of how their bodies work as they "stretch" themselves and their abilities. The painter, photographer, and filmmakers—those who primarily work with form and image—will get a deeper understanding as to what comprises "good" art. In terms of their work, their skills will be sharpened, enabling them to carry out their projects as they couldn't before.

When you begin to discover these changes in your abilities, it can be a very "heady" experience. The joy of creating will become so intense you'll never want to leave it alone. The problem with this mindset is that you could very easily begin to shut yourself off from others, which is very dangerous.

That's when the Holy Spirit has to step in and remind you that there are those who can use you. This is especially true for those of us with families. Creative people have been known to get so wrapped up in what they're doing that it consumes them, which is not necessarily a bad thing. However, when the musician becomes obsessed with developing a new sound or style, depression can ensue when that new thing remains elusive. A better, more balanced sense of who we are and our innate needs (such as the companionship of others) is necessary for us all to grow and flourish.

More and More Fruit

In loving ourselves and our neighbors, we won't be able to escape loving them without heavy doses of faithfulness and gentleness. On the human side of things, we all want these things, and they can even be seen as mundane, commonplace qualities. The truth of the matter is that these are not natural tendencies for the human being. It is easier to be cruel and indifferent than it is to be gentle and faithful. These are lessons, supposedly, learned at our mother's knee.

And I again I have to reiterate: the supernatural fruit of God's Holy Spirit cannot be matched or compared with any earthly conception. As we continue to allow the Spirit to lead us into all truth, we will learn how to show faithfulness and gentleness to those around us. It won't be what we think is the way to do it; it will be His way.

Joy?

The *Book of Lamentations* has a rather dubious title. When one is in a lamentable frame of mind, they are not in the happiest state. Yet, therein lies some verses that can inspire joy in whatever state of mind you may hold. Just as the author wrote many years ago,

> My soul has been continually reminded (of my bad times) and is bowed down within me. And yet, I can remember, I still possess hope and expectation. It is not the Lord's mercies and loving-kindness that are

consumed because His compassion doesn't fail. His generous and abundant mercies are *new* every morning. (Lam. 3:20-23, my paraphrase).

Praise God! His joy doesn't have to be predicated on something I've done, for He gives it freely and liberally, just like His love.

Chapter 4

The Artist's Community

During one industry course I partook in, a number of seasoned Broadway vets taught about "Making It" in the business. One of them admonished us on the necessity of growing as individuals. He stressed the importance of "Community." Oh, no doubt, in the course of putting a show on its feet, we will bond with our fellow players, but there's a lot more at stake. Once the run is over, the reason for our camaraderie ceases to hold us together. Chalk it up to one of the strict realities of life; all of us have to lead our own lives.

Most of us have personal tastes in books, clothes, food, and movies that have filled up our lives since our ten little toes first touched terra firma. Some of us may even have families that anchor us to the reality of this world. We all can feel very content with all of these things and yet, every one of us has a deep rooted, undeniable need for God in our very being.

This is, undoubtedly, not news to many of us who spend our Sunday mornings in various places of worship. My experience has been that there are a growing number of churches that are reaching out to those in the arts world.

Some have support groups and activities that aid in bolstering us "denizens" of creativity.

The trouble is that these artist-friendly holy places are too few in number, partially because the ancient attitudes toward artists still exist. Some churches require that we conform to their ideas concerning artistry. (What we produce has to have some form of "Christian" value or a certain number of Scriptures, somebody has to "see the light" at the end, etc.) Then, there are those who don't seem to care to understand the artistic temperament because the theater (i.e. Hollywood, etc.) is considered entirely "sinful" as well as frivolous.

In a way, I wish this fact was part of the deep, unenlightened past, but not necessarily. In fact, this fact was "rammed" onto my psyche just this past Thanksgiving. While working at a ministry to feed the homeless, I told a young lady that I was unable to attend church because I was performing in a show. She then said she would "pray for me" as if I were in need of deliverance from some sort of demon. Despite any progress in providing a haven for artists, my concern is for the individual.

While many Christian actors and the like (dancers, singers, writers, stage hands, etc.) are seeking refuge in churches, I believe they are missing out on the full life in Christ. They may have a handle on the "essentials," but they don't have a total grasp on all they can have in God.

Called out

According to the Greek definition of *church*, we are "called out" from the world's way of doing things. In the *Book of Acts*, the early Christians banded together and what they had was shared amongst them. The needs of the poor, orphans, widows, and infirmed were met. All of this came about after the infilling of the Holy Spirit "diffused throughout their souls" (Acts 2:4), imbuing them with God's supernatural love for one another.

This whole idea of reaching out to others shouldn't be anything new to us. It is the entire message of the *Bible*, bar none! When we have God's kind of love, it is impossible not to show it off. There are many churches throughout the world that are meeting God's mandate to reach our neighbors. On one hand, I praise God for the innumerous efforts being made. Yet, on the other, I am more than convinced that, our modern day church has missed the mark in too many ways and opportunities.

Building Blocks

The age-old adage is that "it takes a village to raise a child." The pure thrust of the idea behind it is that there are many individuals who are involved, but even before the child enters this life, we need these other folks to come together as a committed group. Each person is an integral part of it. The trouble is that there are some weak links in that chain of people. In spite of any weaknesses they may possess, they can still be part of it all. We have to be built up.

I have a song to sing-o

As I've already brought up in the first chapter, I love to sing! While breathing can be a normal, ordinary occurrence for a wide majority of the populace, it can be an absolute thrill for me. Whether or not all people who sing feel the same way is hard to say, for I've never heard any such sentiment from the many I've known.

Oh sure, throughout my life, I've met scads and scads of folks who love to sing. At the drop of the proverbial hat, they'll let loose with a song or two wherever and whenever they can find an audience. The spotlight is on them, and they love to bask in the warmth of those listening. The trouble is, nine times out of ten, at least eight of those singers can't sing! There's no technique, no musical finesse or talent. The majority of them couldn't hold on to a tune if their lives depended on it. To me, these people are not *singers*.

The general population would be in steadfast disagreement with me, for there is a pervasive belief that all people can sing. I'm sorry, but it just isn't so. Plainly put, there are *singers*, and then there are people who sing. The singers, the true artists, are the ones who have spent hours, compelled to develop their voices.

Our American society throws the word *talent* around like so many molecules of oxygen in the air. Just about everyone and anyone who can dance a step or carry a tune is considered to have talent. However, talent is more elusive than the majority of people know. There is a great difference between being gifted with a talent and having the ability to do something. In other words, not all people who have a singing lead role in a musical qualify as singers. Likewise, the person who strides the boards of a stage is not necessarily an actor.

"Talent" is what shuts you away to work on your craft or whatever that gifting may be. It is what compels you to go from one level to the next. An actor such as Sir Lawrence Olivier will be just as adept at comedy as he is with drama. A rock singer with the depth of Freddie Mercury would be able to sing arias in Carnegie Hall. The writer may fall more in love with the power of words and dare to explore different ways of expressing themselves. The guitar player with only three major chords under their belt will be inspired to learn the beauty of major sevenths and the dissonance of flatted fifths.

An Idea that Bears Repeating

Okay, it's not that I want to sound like I'm talking out of both sides of my mouth, but when it comes to performances, there's always room for everybody. There is that necessary blend of people who may not sing as well as others. Ensembles will always need town people of all shapes, sizes, and ages to speak lines and sing the choruses.

The trouble comes when the artists wrap their lives in their abilities. Deep down, they feel that this is how they get their recognition as well as their reason to exist and survive, but this is no foundation to build a life upon. Such a false notion in one's well-being can only lead to a life of inner turmoil and heartache.

A true and honest life assessment can only come from God, and it's what we all need to strive for. We must endure the pain of honestly seeing our shortcomings and blunders. The greatest thing about being honest about our failures, our mistakes, is the realization that *we're all* essentially alike, and we all need each other.

> The body created by God is a master work of engineering. Not only do we all have fingers, shoulders, knees, and toes there is a foundational frame. On that frame is a system of "levers" and joints made up of muscles and sinew. Every part has its purpose and is all made to work together. So it is with us human beings. We're all here to complement one another. (1 Cor. 12:12)

Don't limit yourself

When we prefer to focus on what we do to define ourselves, we run the risk of restricting all that we're capable of being. It's sort of like a diet of only hot dogs and pizza. We would be missing out on all the great flavors and delicacies the world has to offer.

Perhaps you have facility with languages, a keen ear for accents. Such traits can open up a whole bunch of life-enhancing opportunities, such as teaching English as a second language or even coaching other actors in the art of shaping a particular dialect. Don't neglect your intellect!

"Well, ya got to have friends!"

Those of us in the artistic temperament community can be notorious for spending a lot of time within ourselves. It is a practice that can be very "off-putting," social-wise, making us appear unfriendly and even strange.

On the one hand, it is a very necessary trait, for it aids in the creative process. Hours and sometimes days will pass when I'm in my self-imposed oblivion as I flip ideas back and forth, mentally organizing and choreographing them into a form that pleases me. Even as an actor, I'll disappear into my thoughts, going over my lines. The "leetle gray cells" that make up my brain will be full of bits of business (shtick) meant to enhance my performance.

While time in seclusion is a good and necessary trait, I'd better not remain in that state of an "island unto myself." I eventually have to come out my mental exile because somebody is going to need me for whatever reason. Just as the human frame needs toes to stand erect, it is not good for man (or woman) to be alone as it is said in the second chapter of *Genesis*.

It doesn't fail! Whatever show I'm engaged in, the young folks always manage to clump together. And, why not? They share a lot more in common with each other than those 10 to 15 years older. In spite of any age differences, career goals, or even gross shyness, we have to work together. We have to make some form of an effort to get along.

Of course, there's a transient aspect of the artistic world (show business, in particular). The majority of the relationships we do make are of a tenuous and superficial nature. Therefore, we feel reluctant to get close to anyone, which is more than understandable. However, as Christians, we are commanded to love those around us. In fact, after spending time in God's presence, you will feel compelled to do so.

The Wholly Church

Just before the famous love chapter (1 Corinthians 13) begins, Paul writes, "Now you (collectively) are Christ's body and (individually) you are members of it, each part severally and distinct—each with his own place and function" (1 Cor. 12:27). Prior to that statement, he writes, "And if one member suffers all the parts [share] the suffering" (1 Cor. 12:26).

In no uncertain terms, we are all inextricably bound together, whether we like it or not. Being in the body means we have a God-given responsibility to one another. The problem is that the majority of our brothers and sisters either don't know it, or don't care to.

This whole chapter of Paul's First Epistle to the Corinthians is about how the body of Christ is supposed to work. Special roles are meted out to each member so that the work of the body can be carried out. Many church denominations don't teach about the jobs within the body, relegating them a deep, dark distant past.

Therefore, the claim of ignorance can be made by a good majority of Christians. It can even be said that these are "babes in Christ," for they have yet to chew on the meat of the God's message. Whatever the qualifying statement, it's a sad commentary indeed, for the body of Christ is dying due to immaturity.

As I grew in my Christian life, I would look at the words of the Great Commission: "Go then and make disciples of all the nations" (Matt. 28:19) and say it was for somebody else to do. The office of evangelist just was not mine, but then I grew in the faith by chewing on that good news meat and found out differently.

It may not be my "calling" to go from town to town, standing on street corners, shouting out the gospel, but there is so much I need to do. Connecting with my brothers and sisters on a meaningful level and not just on a casual, Sunday sort of way is the main consideration.

It has been such a total blessing when I've been in a strange church and worshiping with others who are mature in their faith. This is something I've experienced in several different cities and countries. There was an overwhelming "coming home" feeling present. Many of these strangers would warmly greet me, calling me, "Brother."

The biggest deterrent in our maturation is fear. You may feel, as I did, that it just isn't your place to reach out, which is very understandable. Maybe there's an extreme shyness that has been a telling characteristic your whole life. But, believe me, I am no super-extroverted type person myself. We really don't need to be some sort of super saint. You may feel it's really tough (maybe even excruciating) but more than possible.

Do unto others

The smallest actions on our parts can help break the ice as well as maintain life in the body of Christ. Little things like getting to know the other person's name can be the first step in the right direction. (If it's a "foreign" name, it'll be a plus when you show you've made the effort to pronounce it correctly.) Listening is another great contributor to growth. If it's a fellow performer, and they do something you really like, let them know you appreciate it.

Be an encourager

Encouragement is such a necessary gift to cultivate, especially when you're out in that "cold, cruel" artistic world. One of the best ways to compliment somebody is to say something you'd like to hear yourself. If you're a singer, and you honesty like the way somebody else sings, you can let them know that. Of course, the sentiment will not necessarily be reciprocated (too many times, my compliments have been met with all the warmth of Mount Rushmore), but you may not know what sort of personal doors can be opened.

Be available for people

In this Facebook/Twitter world we occupy, making "friends" and networking has become very easy. It's all so very enticing to be able to reach out to so many people all over the globe. My biggest hang up with Facebook (as well as with e-mail in general) is that a lot of those I've befriended lack a generous amount of courtesy. Too many times, when I've been on the site, my queries seem to be ignored. There is usually little to no response from my "friends." Not veddy nice at all!

I am more than convinced that we believers need to go that extra mile (Matt. 5:41) and not join in what everybody else is doing. Nobody likes to be ignored. Everybody deserves to be treated as we would want to be. Going that extra mile requires us to step out of our comfort zones, which can be scary.

The reverse side of that fear is that it can be rewarding when we make an effort. Say somebody gives you something you really liked. Don't fail to let them know. If you can offer a deeper explanation as to why you liked it, that couldn't hurt.

Pray for others

Then, of course, there's prayer! Approaching someone (be they Christian or not) and letting them know that you care enough for them to bring them before the throne of God is a double plus! You could just pray for them "at a distance," but it doesn't hurt to be a bit more personal. In terms of your brothers and sisters, we are admonished to gather together and share our weaknesses with one another (Jam. 5:16). Being honest about our imperfections and struggles shows that we're real and not some kind of spiritual automatons. Those are the times when prayer is needed so badly. The love of God really shines through when prayer is declared!

Chapter 5

The Artist's Devotion

A large majority of church-going believers have spent a significant portion of their lives in places they were introduced to as children. It's part of their family's religious heritage; therefore, they are Christians. This would include those who subscribe to an evangelical frame of mind. Not only have they attended their parents' church for years, they also adhere to the doctrine that a Christian is someone who has been "born again." They have made that definitive declaration personally to accept Jesus Christ as their personal Lord and Savior.

In spite of any wide doctrinal differences between denominations, the majority of these Christians believe that their lives should be characterized by the Biblical mandates of abstinence from excessive alcohol, foul language, and pre- and extramarital sex. They also know that they are to refrain from lying, cheating their neighbors, coveting their neighbor's property, and stealing.

Some religious communities have augmented the list with their church's own "shalt nots." These ecclesiastical places stress the avoidance of theatrical performances (both stage and film), social dancing, and reading questionable literature. Some of them also forbid women from wearing make-up.

So zealous are some groups in their belief systems that their lives consist of long lists of dos and don'ts. One big problem with this mindset is that it confines life to a set of rules. This is the bare essence of what makes up a religion, which is not what God had in mind for anyone who believes in Him. From the very dawn of time, He has sought man to be in relationship with Him.

Freedom!

In the very first chapters of *Genesis*, we can see how God reached out to His final and best creation. He placed Adam and Eve in a paradise where all of their needs were provided for from day one. They had no need to fear the animals around them. Neither did they have to worry about clothes or food. They had it made in the proverbial shade!

To add to their comfort, God would come and spend time with the couple. The evidence of their special communion is made more than evident in the third chapter. So ashamed after their act of disobedience, they hid themselves. Any semblance of peace had left them because their close relationship had been immediately severed. It was the consequence of their sin.

The eighth verse of this chapter reveals the kind of relationship God shared with the first couple. As they cowered together, they could hear "the sound of the Lord God walking in the garden in the cool of the day" (Gen.

3:8). This is such a cool, "wow moment." I can't help but be totally floored and amazed by the shear scope of it all. In a way, it reminds me of my relationship with my mother.

Growing up, I can recollect hearing my Mom approach my bedroom. She always wore these bracelets that would clang and jangle when she walked. So, depending on the situation (whether I was good or bad), it was (sometimes) a comfort to know she was coming. Her clang and jangle was undoubtedly just as familiar to me as God's "sound" to Adam and Eve. They had apparently spent a good amount of time together for them to make that so very distinct recognition.

Even after having been expelled from their place of comfort, the relationship continues. Adam and Eve instructed their children, Cain and Abel, on the importance of making sacrifices to God. This was the covenant between God and His creation. Unfortunately, as seen in the subsequent, fourth chapter of *Genesis*, Cain shows his contempt for God in his offering and is, therefore, rejected.

In the twelfth chapter of *Genesis*, God seeks out and makes an explicit covenant with Abram (the pre-Abraham of Genesis 17:5). From his loins, would spring a people whom God would bless forever, and from this chosen people, the whole world would be blessed.

Hundreds of years later (in the book of Exodus) at the foot of a desert mountain, thousands of Abraham's descendants have come to a rest. After having been rescued from brutal enslavement, they have walked hundreds of miles. By day, their Lord and God has guided them with a cloud. The night sky saw a pillar of fire in the cloud's place.

Not only that but both food and water were miraculously provided for His people.

Their leader, Moses, has been acting as the immediate mediator throughout the trip. At one point, the Lord God tells his servant that He wants to explain to his people that He wants them to come closer to Him. The very specific instructions were that they had to clean their clothes and that they could come to the mountain. However, they could not climb up or even touch the "border of it" under penalty of death.

On that auspicious day, thunder boomed and lightning crackled. From a thick cloud, these Children of Israel heard the sound of a loud trumpet, and they were more than understandably scared. In spite of this, God wanted them to come to Mount Sinai.

During some alone time, Moses reminded the Almighty that He had admonished the people that they could not cross the boundary line He had set up. The prophet was then told to go back to those waiting and tell them everything He had to say to them. This marked the first time anyone had ever heard of God's Ten Commandments.

In the subsequent centuries, God spoke to His people through his prophets. It was in their numerous warnings and admonitions that God expressed His love to his wayward Chosen. Even during the time of severe chastisement, He would raise up those who would remind them of His unfailing commitment. Obviously (from the various books of the Old Testament), the Children of Israel became tired of the doom-saying messengers, and many of these prophets were murdered by their hands.

Thankfully, God didn't just abandon these descendants of Abraham. He sent His Son not to condemn the world, but that all may come to saving knowledge of Him. Throughout His ministry, Jesus said that He and the Father were one and that he was all about doing His will. Jesus exclaimed His Father's love for the Jewish people when he stated,

> O Jerusalem, Jerusalem, murdering prophets and stoning them who are sent to you! How often I would have gathered your children together as a mother fowl gathers her under her wings, and you refused. (Matt. 23:37)

Despite His innumerable and consistent advances toward His people, we continue to keep our distance. With our many doctrines and church duties, we have derived a measure of comfort. Psychologists have established that children thrive on routine, a disposition that most human beings never grow out of. There's a certain satisfaction, even serenity, in going through the same job every day, eating the same foods, and then returning to the same bed every evening.

Unfortunately, one big problem with routine is that it breeds complacency. It can be that comfy chair we find difficult to extricate ourselves from at the end of the day. We don't want to be moved. We'd rather not be bothered. Undoubtedly, it is very nice, but there's no growth or challenge in that sort of lifestyle. We are all built to do and accomplish more in our lives.

Jesus said that He came to give us an abundant life. It is in Him where we find that "more." And you can believe this: it's not something that suddenly comes "upon" us. It's just like with anything worthwhile in life. Whether it be running a race or sewing, it takes diligence and effort on our part.

The Big Two

The authorities of His day were always trying to trip up Jesus in order to gain some negative evidence against him. So a lawyer, (not the modern-day take-you-to-court-and-sue-you type) an expert in the Mosaic Law, approached Him. His pointed inquiry was, "What is the greatest commandment?" Without blinking an eye, the Lord replied, "Love the Lord your God with all of your heart, mind and soul. This is the greatest commandment." Continuing, He said,

> The second most important is similar: Love your neighbor as yourself. All the other commandments and all the demands of the prophets that stem from these two laws are fulfilled if you obey them. Keep only these and you will find you are obeying all the others. (Matt. 22:37-40, my paraphrase)

This is an absolutely amazing statement, so succinct in content and concise in its message. All 66 books of the Bible (except for most of the historical narrative portions) can be summed in these few lines. While the Ten Commandments were not given to mankind until centuries into our existence, we knew what God expected of us, for it was written into our hearts. God made it so that the "invisible things" and even his "external power" could be clearly recognized (Rom. 1:20). Therefore, we would be without any excuse when it came to knowing what was right and wrong.

Notable testaments to this fact are the many codes of societal conduct that have been held by so many people throughout our world's history. These societies knew that, if they were going to survive, they would have to establish some set of rules that would regulate people's behavior. There would have to be some way to deter stealing, killing, and lying, or they would not be able to live in any semblance of peace.

More specifically, when it comes to the Ten Commandments, the first four deal with the love of God. For us to truly love God, we would have to recognize Him as our God and not have any other god in our lives, nor would we make any sort of objects of wood or stone to replace Him. His name is to be important to us, not something said in a frivolous or casual manner. The Sabbath Day, set aside as His day, would have to be observed as we determine to rest in Him.

The remaining six Commandments concern themselves loving those around us. This, of course, refers to honoring and respecting our parents. We are not to think so little of our neighbors that we would want them dead.

We should not think so little of our families (and the families of our neighbors) that we would take another's spouse. To steal, lie, and covet somebody else's property (relationship) is a sure way to end up devastated.

While we in the Christian Church have not failed to fill our catechisms and lexicons with these lessons throughout the centuries, we have not learned their importance. No doubt, many a parishioner can rifle off the tenets paramount to what they believe, but it's primarily head knowledge. The practicality, the intent of God's words, has escaped us.

God didn't intend for the Ten Commandments just to be memorized. They were to safeguard every man's dignity. They were to ensure that all men and women (not just the Hebrew children) would be treated with respect. This is one of the many blessings all of mankind would receive from Abraham's covenant.

We Go Together

An important fact we've missed is that the two "Big" commandments work in tandem. You can't have one without the other. In other words, you can't learn what it is to truly love who you are until you love God as He wants us to.

Ay, there's the rub! There's no doubt in my mind that if I was standing in a room of Christians and asked if they loved God, the majority would not be afraid to declare in the affirmative. In fact, I'm reminded of a time when I was off to a retreat. We all piled into a van, all excited for this opportunity to be away with our brothers and sisters.

The driver, jubilant fellow that he was, turned to us asking, "Who wants to go to heaven?" We all, of course, chimed in enthusiastically. Then, in a mock sinister tone, he said, "Who wants to go now?" The comical retort was met with a bit of laughter, but there was also a hint of uneasiness because we had no idea who this guy really was.

When it comes to the things of God, most of us want to be counted with everybody else. None of us wants to be that odd man (or woman) out. And yet, like those of us occupying the speeding van, we all need to learn what we're committing ourselves to.

What could be the possible cost? We have to learn to love God by His standards and not our own. Finding out that God's concept of love wouldn't match what we already know shouldn't really surprise us because the prophet Isaiah tell us God's thoughts are not on the same plane as ours (Isa. 55:8). It wouldn't be wrong for me to mention that we have to defer to His thoughts if we want that peace the world doesn't give (John 14:27).

God's Kinda Love

The next, most logical question would be, "How do we find out about God's sort of love?" The Bible says that the God kinda love…

...is persistent and consistent; never gives up. Is patient and kind, never envious; cares more for others than one's self. Is not proud or rude. Is not self seeking; does not insist on its own way. Is not touchy; overly sensitive. Does not keep score of wrongs done. Does not rejoice in injustice but rejoices in truth and just causes. (1 Cor. 13:4-7)

Other examples of how God looks at love can be found in the fifth chapter of *Matthew*. Thinking so little of someone that you call them any kind of demeaning name is enough to court heaven's wrath. Our relationships with our brothers and sisters (our neighbors) are so important to God that we are to do whatever we can do to make things right.

Therefore, we are to be emphatically honest in what we say. Since we wouldn't want somebody saying things to us just to be "polite," we shouldn't do it to them either. After all, it is really duplicitous (two-faced, forked-tongued) of us if we say "yes" with shades of maybe. The same goes for the kind of "no" we use. Being forthcoming in our communication can protect us against a lot of embarrassment and hurt feelings.

Then, there's the "beyond the call" aspect of God's love. When we're asked to do anything, whether it be ironing a shirt or carrying somebody's laundry, our attitude should be one of willingness. To ask if there's anything we can possibly do (even if it be giving somebody your shirt or walking that extra mile) is, perhaps, a bit scary, but it doesn't have to be. Many a time, it's nice just to hear the offer.

Our human kinda love

On another one of those occasions when the temple authorities tried to trip up Jesus, a Pharisee asked Him if there was a "legal" reason for a man to divorce his wife. The Lord knew just who He was dealing with; He knew the man's heart intent. His explanation was, because Moses was more than familiar with man's hard-hearted nature, a concession was made. The husband was to give his wife "a bill of divorcement" in order to obtain his divorce.

The implications are staggering. A man could be married to a woman for a few years, find her disagreeable for whatever reason, and want to divorce her. His most probable reason for exercising this "right" was that he saw another woman he wanted to marry.

A cold-hearted, insensitive, selfish desire that would bring no good to those he lived with. Any consideration of his wife's feelings and emotional welfare is totally absent in his intent. The spouse and children cease to have any relevance and, therefore, can be cast aside. This is why God hates divorce.

When reading today's headlines or listening to just about any news report, it's more than apparent that the heart of man hasn't changed. Celebrities that marry only to give up their respective spouses a short while later (whether it be months, weeks, or days) show they have no idea of what love truly is.

This is even true just for people's own bodies. If they don't like parts of their bodies, they can have it lifted, nipped, or tucked away. These parts of God's Creation bring them disfavor and, therefore, are dispensable. The same can be said of the modern trend of piercings and tattoos. For many, the human body is something to be trashed.

Our human, worldly type of love is superficial, cowardly, irresponsible, and temporary. What God has to offer is gloriously better and much more satisfying.

How Do We Love God?

So, what does it actually mean to love God? From a human standpoint, it is immeasurably easier to love someone, something that we can see and feel. Children learn to love from the people who raise them. Those times when the parent comforted the child in times of sorrow, or just plain, everyday moments of meeting their basic needs—food, clothing, and warmth—are all examples of this love. In that environment of security, they learn what it is to be loved and to return love.

However, it is obviously not the same when it comes to God. God's very essence is not of a solid entity. He is Spirit, neither male nor female. His residence is not here on earth. He doesn't live in some lofty, impenetrable castle. He dwells in the place known as heaven.

Several instances in the Bible make it clear that it is more than dangerous to be near Him. Seeing the burning bush, Moses was instructed to take off his shoes and not to get too close. When it comes to love, God is not someone we humans can readily "cuddle up" to. And yet, we come by this love in a different way.

The famous faith verse, Hebrews 11:1, states emphatically that it is impossible to please God without faith. It goes on to say that we (anyone) who want to truly approach Him must be convinced that "He exists and that He cares enough to respond to those who seek him" (11:6).

Earlier in the chapter, the writer points out that our Biblical ancestors rose above those they lived with because their faith in God was what distinguished them. People such as Enoch, Noah, and Abraham knew that their God was someone to be reckoned with.

Faith, like love, is a verb; it requires action on our part. If we love someone, we want to do things for them; we want to be near and with them. So it should be with the Lord, for He is our Creator. He is our beginning and end, the Alpha and Omega. Fear and reverence toward God is where we start with our love for Him.

One of my all-time favorite verses is Psalm 37:4, which says, "Delight yourself in the Lord and he shall give you the desires and the secret petitions of your heart." Of course, that whole part about receiving the desires of your heart is a powerful incentive to "love" Him, but it is not enough. Children who love their parents only because they give them everything they want will not rise above the maturity level of children. This is an unbalanced, selfish relationship that really doesn't stand a chance to survive. Parties on both sides will feel cheated.

When we *delight* in someone, just being around them is a total pleasure. We seek them out so that the pleasure will go on for as long as it can. We want to know what it is that will please them. In fact, just thinking about them can be a total source of enjoyment. I can't remember how many times when the thought of a loved one brought a wide smile to my face and a few tears here and there. Or, how 'bout those times when mere words failed to explain what was in my heart. Songs were the only adequate expressions for what lay therein. It can be that way with the Lord.

How Can I Keep from Singing

A large majority of Christian hymns were written as expressions of what was in their writers' hearts. Starting with the writers of the Psalms, they exposed their needs, their love, and their confidence in God for the whole world to witness. Their desire to reach the heart of God was more than evident.

> Listen to my words, O Lord; give heed to my *sighing* and groaning. Hear the sound of my cry, my king and my God, for to You do I pray. In the morning you hear my voice, O Lord; in the morning I prepare a prayer of sacrifice to you." (Psa. 5:1-3)

Why can't we all do the same? I don't mean writing hymns or praise choruses (even though that wouldn't hurt). I'm referring to the revealing, *voicing* part of the equation. These writers, these saints, laid down some mighty footsteps we can follow. Here's a mighty, jumping-off point!

Certainly, when we start learning to love God, it doesn't and can't stay the same. It must grow and mature like all things in life that have any worth or value. After all, fruit ripens from buds, and babies grow from embryos to full-grown adults. That which fails to improve with age is stunted, impaired in its usefulness. It must grow in order to thrive.

More than once, I've heard the comparison that faith is like a muscle, a body organ that is in need of exercise in order for it to be built up and strengthened. The more we work on it, the stronger it becomes with time. Nothing good or lasting happens overnight.

Therefore, we have to learn about a God kinda love continually so we can know what He expects of us. The key to it all is our willing spirits that want to be intimate with Him. Yet, as with just about everything in life, it can be a two-step dance of two advances forward and one step back. We may slip and fall at times, but He will always be there to pick us up.

Praise and worship

Okay, so all of you of keen-minded and open-spirited people undoubtedly are asking, "Just how do we begin to find out this God kinda love?" My answer is very simple and straight-forward: praise and worship! This is all you need to start yourself on this wondrous journey that will expand your world, blow your mind, and sustain you throughout the rest of your lives.

You may say, "Praise and worship? I've been doing it all of my life. When I was a young kid, I was put on my mother's knee, and we praised and worshiped God." This is not what I'm talking about. While coming together with other believers is undoubtedly a great thing and a good start, there's a whole lot more to it all. Here, let me tell you how I made this life-altering discovery.

Upon returning to New York (having been away at graduate school), I began attending a church I had stumbled over while job hunting. It was quite large. The sanctuary accommodated at least 500 people. While I was more than glad to become a part of the congregation, I was reticent to "join" in with everything. Part of the reason for my feelings was I just didn't want to assimilate into a "group mentality." Most of my fellow congregants liked the same kind of worship music and would recommend it to me. As I said, I was reluctant, and it's not that it was "bad." I just found these types of choruses simplistic.

My guard remained up until one Sunday when I heard the pianist riffing through this Latin, Salsa type of intro. Not only was it rhythmically complex, it was downright catchy. Immediately, I was sent to my feet and began to dance uncontrollably. (What can I say? Good music has that effect on me!) I simply could not keep still. The name of the song was "(He Turns My) Mourning into Dancing," and it was nothing like I had ever heard before in a church. My life-long interest in new music took over, and I had to have it for myself (recording wise). Lo and behold, it was one of those worship albums everybody else was listening to. My rock solid wall of reticence was slowly crumbling.

Another aspect of my stubborn obstinacy was the fact that I knew I was already "very good" at worship. I had quite a few praise albums in my collection. But, when I got my own copy of this particular album, I just about wore it out. I would play it on my way to work and on my way back. I played it on my way to church and on the way back (you get the idea). Even when I exercised, the video of the recording was on in front of my *Nordictrack* ski thingee, inducing a consistent beat that kept my legs pumping.

Slowly but surely, I began to recognize some very subtle changes in the way I worshipped in the church. I found myself to be "freer" in my expression. Being a part of the corporate time of praise was addicting, and I just had to have more. So, I started buying up just about every new worship CD I could find. It had just about taken over my heart and mind.

One day, as I was standing in line at a music store, I began to think about how great it would be to also have the hymns I had learned so many years ago. These songs— such as "How Great Thou Art," "Blessed Assurance," and "Great Is Thy Faithfulness"—all spoke to my heart in such a deep way. They had all already stood the test of time. They were part of the "bulwark never failing" as Martin Luther once wrote.

Praise and worship were now a daily part of my life. As I had just mentioned, I had been listening to Christian music for a good part of my Christian life, and yet phase of my life was just *too* different. From the time when I first heard those simulated Latin strains, I've began telling just about every Christian I meet of the benefits of daily worship.

Further on... into the breach!

Now, I've got a bit of a confession. My personal bias, my personal inclination, is a charismatic, free and open sort of worship. I have found this is the best way to access the throne of grace. All of you whose eyes have glanced over these last few words are undoubtedly thinking, "But I'm Baptist! (or) "I'm Catholic, Presbyterian, Methodist, etc... And our worship is just fine. I'm not joining any hand-raising, tongue-speaking, or jumping-in-aisles kind of service for love or money!" Truth is, you really don't have to. As you probably know, you can still worship God right where you are.

During one of my daily times in the Bible, I came across the familiar story of Jesus and the woman at the well. It was already a favorite of mine, but my eyes got stuck on it that morning. Toward the end of the story, the pair began to have a theological discussion. She pointed out that it was because of Samaritan tradition that they worshiped at Mount Gerizim. The Samaritan woman might as well have said, "Well we're Congregationalists and our worship..." Nevertheless, Jesus really wasn't there for a religious debate, and He knew it really didn't matter what the doctrinal differences were. "The time will come," He said, when God's true (genuine) believers will worship Him in spirit and truth.

I believe very firmly that when we seek with our whole heart, mind, and soul, He will direct us into that path of Spirit and Truth. The Bible says, "Then you will seek Me, inquire and require Me (as a vital necessity) and find me; when you search for Me with all your heart" (Jer. 29:13).

When you do seek God with all your heart, you will find so many changes in your beliefs and attitudes when you firmly divest yourselves in Him. Denomination and sectarian walls will crumble as you learn to embrace His Spirit and truth. If I haven't said it once, I will say it at least fifteen times: it is so important to develop a daily habit of praise and worship. *The benefits are astounding!* You can't lose by engaging in it. It can be oh so very simple.

In this grossly portable music world we live in, there are so many helps in that direction. There are iPods, iPhones, cassette players (the old standby relics), CD players, and my personal favorite, the Discmans.

Your choice of music has also been made affordable with tons of variety. Just to name a few, there are the popular praise choruses, total praise albums like those of Darlene Zschech and Ron Kenoly. No doubt, you'll be able to find the music in your preferred languages and styles. Then, just like food, it doesn't help to just stare at it once you have it; you have to consume it. Better yet, let it consume you.

Back to basics

Here, let me backtrack just a bit. While I feel praise and worship is extremely important to one's spiritual growth, there are other elements that also very necessary. Let's start off with...

Prayer

At the end of *A Chorus Line,* the Pulitzer Prize-winning musical, the cast sings the song "What I Did For Love." The love they are referring to has little to nothing to do with the love between two people. It's about all of the hard work they've put into learning their trade—the hours spent in mastering their craft, whether it was learning a song, an intricate piece of choreography, or their lines for a scene. Not to mention, all of the other heartaches they've had to put up with during their careers.

The song is also about the pain they've put themselves through—whether that pain be physical or emotional, real or imaginary. Whatever work they've done has brought them to where they are. They know, in spite of any amount of success they've achieved, it has come because of all the work they've put into it all. Nothing has come easy. So, the same thing can be said about prayer.

Believe it or not, some people don't know how to pray. Oh, no doubt, they know prayer is: essentially, it's communicating with God. Problem is, they really haven't advanced out of the habit of treating God like a cosmic sugar daddy. "Yes, Lord, give me this, that, and the other thing because I need it." And, unfortunately, it doesn't go any farther than this partially because they're scared or have yet to mature out of the realm of children. It's fine to start there but God wants more for us.

According to Richard Foster, author of *Celebration of Discipline,* "To pray is to change. Prayer is the central avenue God uses to transform us."[1] Starting off a day in prayer is much akin to that all very important first meal. It can do wonders in determining how your day goes.

The sixth chapter of *Matthew* gives Christ's admonition on how to pray. He starts by telling us that we are to "enter into our closet and shut the door." In other words, we are not to be very "show-offy" in what we do. The Lord then goes on to say we are to pray in this manner:

Praise - Our Father in heaven, may your name receive all the praise and honor it deserves. Your Holy and precious will be done in my life, on the earth just as it is in Heaven.

Supplication for our needs - Your word states that you know every one of my needs before I even have to ask. So please, supply to me everything I need for this day: food, encouragement, love, and peace.

Intercession - Don't let my failings and short comings be held against me in your eyes. In fact, keep my eyes, ears, and heart open to you so that I may learn what I shouldn't do. And just as you forgive me, give me the heart to overlook all the slights and unkind things done by others.

Protection - Let me not yield to temptation so that it doesn't overcome me, and deliver me from the snares and barbs of the evil one for I surely don't need his company.

This way of praying can be a useful tool, for it not only lends a certain structure, but you also have a good deal of freedom. For example, in the first part, you can throw in as many worshipful phrases as you like. During your time of laying out your petitions (your needs) you can let Him know how you're feeling: all of those fears, moments of heartache and anguish.

Once you've got all those things off your mind, you can get down to the real nitty-gritty and seek forgiveness for anything you may have done. Then, you can go on to pray for friends, family—whatever needs there may be. Last, but not least, you can pray for that "hedge of protection" as you go about your day.

Just as an arm or leg muscle is strengthened by the exercise of said muscles, so it goes with the "prayer" muscle. Let us, "Pray without ceasing" (1 Thess. 5:17), for the, "prayer of a righteous man avails much" (Jam. 5:16).

Fasting

This may not be the easiest discipline to conquer, but it is very necessary. Richard Foster's take is that it assists in keeping our lives in balance. Fasting can help us see the things in life that can control us, whether they be food or even emotions (pride). Other benefits are: 1) an increased effectiveness in praying for others, 2) guidance in decision-making, 3) increase in concentration, 4) deliverance for those in bondage, 5) physical well-being, and 6) godly revelations.

Now, there are many ways of fasting. You don't necessarily have to go without food for long periods of time. This is especially true for those who are diabetic or hypoglycemic. One could just skip one meal or even cut out all carbs for a period of time. Then, you could also fast by cutting out all TV. The main thing is that it is all done unto God, or it really won't be worth doing.

My particular favorite is the Daniel Fast, for it really does not lend itself to hardship, especially when it comes to eating. This variation is taken from the pages of the book of Daniel. When taken to live in Babylon, Daniel and his three friends told the king that they would not be eating the same foods of those around them. They were content to eat only products (produce) derived from the ground, that which came from seeds and drinking water.

To some, this would mean concentrating on fruit, which would be very true. I knew of one pastor who liked his "grape" fast, consuming only grapes and grape juice. And yet, such a fast would also include "veggies!" There are so many of those, including grains (oatmeal/rice), legumes (beans) and their by-products (tofu). One can very easily go a whole lifetime on a diet like that. (They call themselves vegetarians, but I just call them nuts.) Oh yes! A wide variety of nuts are also included.

Susan Gregory, author of *The Daniel Fast*, lays it out in a very facile, user-friendly, and guaranteed "un-failable" (if there such a word) way. She maps every detail out for even the faintest of heart. There's a 21-day plan as well as a whole bunch of very tasty recipes. While Daniel himself states that he ate no "pleasant" food (Dan. 10:3), Susan makes it clear fasting does not have to be harsh or boring.

Again, it's all up to individual how they will or won't follow this discipline. The benefits far outweigh the problems, especially when it comes to drawing closer to God and learning how to hear from Him. This, like any other thing done for Him, can be a burden if practiced with an attitude of, "I hafta." Therefore, a cheery and loving heart is a grand prerequisite.

Study

"Thy word is a lamp unto my feet and a light unto my path." (Psa. 119:105)

"Receive, I pray you, the law and instruction from His mouth, and lay up His words in your heart." (Job 22:22)

It is totally impossible to know what God's Word has for us without (reading) studying it. We all don't need to get theological degrees, but it is very necessary to spend time in it. We also don't need to be Biblical scholars. And yet, at the same time, it is important to know what is and what isn't found in the text of God's Word. If somebody were to say to you, "'The Lord helps those who help themselves' is in Hezekiah 13:13," you can look them straight in the eye and say, "Sorry, there is no such book or verse anywhere near the Bible."

Our old friend, Richard Foster, states that there are four steps when it comes to study:

1) Repetition - Helps by specifically focusing our thought life into a particular wave length.
2) Concentration - Helps to center the mind on what is being studied.
3) Comprehension - Brings insight and discernment into what is studied.
4) Reflection - Aides in leading us to see things from God's perspective.

Another aspect of study can be meditation. While the term is largely associated with Eastern religious practices such as Transcendental Meditation, it can, nevertheless, be used in the study of Scripture. When someone meditates (especially you actors), we are compelled to engage our imaginations. We can enter the "scene" of the Scripture. Let's say we are studying the *Psalms*.

Repetition dictates that we come back to read each one. We get to number 23, and our eyes are locked (concentrated) in on the first verse that states, "The Lord is my shepherd." Now, in spite of the fact that you've never been on a farm or out in the country, you should, undoubtedly know that a shepherd herds animals, whether they be goats or sheep. He is not a policeman or a fireman or even a jet pilot. Your comprehension brings past knowledge into play.

Even if you've never been around a shepherd, the next line gives you a strong a clue of what he does. You're not out on a street corner somewhere: "He makes me lie down in *green pastures*." Here's where meditation comes in handy.

It's been a trying day for you. You've gone to five fruitless auditions. If you're a writer, your publisher doesn't like a thing you've written. It just so happens to be the first day of Spring, and you feel like you'd better sit on something soft, or you're just going to have to fall down. You just so happen to be near a park, and you just plop yourself down. The fresh smell of the grass carries you to a time when life was simpler for you, and you begin to relax.

Not only is there a "green pasture," but there's a babbling brook real close by. You're in heaven! As you continue reading the psalm, you come to comprehend about God's desire to bring you peace and comfort.

Repetition is really helpful when it comes to Scripture memorization. Developing this habit can be especially important when you are in need of knowing His promises for life. And to make things easy, you could order such courses where they help to know verses you can use in telling others of your faith, encouragement, and just plain old personal growth. The Navigators' *Topical Memory System* can be a great help in this area.

And so it goes...

Imagination is such a powerful ally in bringing you closer to Him. It can also help in time of praise and worship. Many a time, when I've gone into "my prayer closet" on my way to work, I know I'll be left alone. The earbuds rest in my aural canal, and I can quietly concentrate on the song's words and be led into a meditative time with the Lord.

So many of our hymn writers have made things almost totally easy to make our way before His throne as we contemplate on lyrics such as,

> Oh Lord, my God as I in awesome wonder
> Consider all the worlds thy hands have made.
> I see the stars, I hear the rolling thunder
> Thy power throughout the universe displayed.
> Then sings my soul, my savior God to thee
> How Great Thou art.
> How Great Thou art.

All such words are glorious reminders of what God has done and is more than capable of doing. These words have a tendency to edge their way into our souls. They can bolster us up in times of trouble as we seek Him and His presence. Do this, and you'll never be sorry you started.

The discipline of daily praise and worship in our individual lives is more than important, but so is corporate worship. In the *Book of Hebrews*, we are instructed on the importance of coming together with others to worship.

In her book, *The Prayer That Changes Everything: The Hidden Power of Praising God*, Stormie Omartian sums up this imperative very nicely:

> There's something that happens when we worship God together with other believers... There's a

renewing, reviving and refreshing of own our souls... and when you let yourself be swept up into it, it will melt and change your heart... It is in our own personal worship times that you will develop an intimate relationship with him.[2]

A strong piece of encouragement I need to lay before you is that you really don't need to sing well to have your personal times with God. While I cringe when I hear Christians jokingly admonish those who don't sing well, "Make a joyful noise" (I've heard the joke one too many times), there is some truth to the old chestnut. Don't let your lack of singing prowess stop you in your efforts venture out on your own.

Hard times

The body of Christ throughout the world is dying. Well, it is, at least, in the ICU and in desperate need of resuscitation. Too many of our denominations are stuck in the mire of decades of their traditions. We have spent too much time cloistered away from "sinners," especially in the realm of sexual sin. There are many "Parachurch" organizations formed within the last 20 to 30 years to address such problems. And yet, there is still too much alarming evidence that there is so much work to be done.

What does this all have to do with us? Well, I'll tell ya. It's quite simple. It is very hard to live in this world. To insist we are loving it while not doing anything about what's going on is just plain wrong! Political and economic problems aside, there are multitudes upon multitudes of lost people out there. If we, God's children, firmly believe we know a miracle-working God, we have to be convinced of our calling to reach the lost.

Take a look around you. There are people who are treating their bodies as pin cushions, piercing every part of themselves from top to bottom. If there's not a piece of metal protruding from somewhere, there is some colorful image drawn into their flesh. The specific "whys" of such acts escapes me totally. Maybe it's part of a fad. Maybe it's done to fit in with one's cronies. Perhaps it's done out of boredom. Whatever the reasons, I am not convinced that someone who truly loves themselves will do such things. It all may seem "cool" to you, but it is all a part of a yell for help.

Jesus said, "The harvest is indeed abundant" (Luke 10:2). You probably know many of your fellow artists who are struggling with the many ills of 21st-Century living. They are those creative types who are battling with the effects of compulsive, obsessive, escapist, and addictive behaviors. Illnesses such as Anorexia, Bulimia, alcohol abuse, and drug abuse are all running rampant in the creative community. This includes your fellow Christian artists. We are not immune to such disorders of the soul.

It is so easy to fall into these self-destructive patterns mainly because we truly don't know what it is to love ourselves and love God. Too many times, I've heard Christian testimonies where people spoke about how they purposely cut themselves or indulged in alcohol and drugs because of the deep pain within. They were all "leaning on their own understanding" (Prov. 3:5), trying to assuage the hurts only God can heal.

Sharing the Good News

The old adage states that evangelism is equated to one beggar telling another where to find bread. It is one person caring enough for another's well-being to tell about something to benefit them. So it is with the Good News (The Gospel) of Christ.

While in college, I participated in a Daytona Beach outreach. This enormously fun-filled event took place during a typical spring break. Our main goal was to be amongst the hundreds of thrill seeking students and tell them about God's wonderful plan for their lives.

In preparation for the ministry, we underwent training on bringing our message in a plain and easy way. Campus Crusade's "Four Spiritual Laws" aided in opening a conversation with those we met on the beach. Each booklet of the Laws mapped our way through what could have proven to be some very personal and difficult discussions.

The Campus Crusade approach is only one way to carry the Good News to others. D. James Kennedy's *Evangelism Explosion* is very similar in introducing God's plan. They too have their booklet of ice-breaking, discussion-invoking questions. Both of these ways of evangelism can be very effective methods. For me, they can also be rather intrusive as well as impersonal.

Whatever way you chose to share God's love with others, it is best to do it with those who are willing to listen.

It is also very important to know what you believe. Just as a singer has to be sure of how their breathing affects each note and tone that emanates from their bodies, it is necessary to know what God can do for you.

Nowadays, there is a lot of "spiritual" misinformation floating around in the creative community. Much of it has been taken from the *Bible*. Then, it's been mixed in with a lot of information from other sources. You have New Age beliefs and Eastern Religions with a few personal ideas thrown in for good measure. The word, *spiritual*, has taken on a myriad of meanings and connotations. The admonition of Genesis 1:26 has been turned on its head, for we have made God into *our* own image.

Therefore, it is very important to know what you've been taught, but it is also important to know where others are coming from. To simply "witness" (evangelize, sharing God's Good News) to someone you met yesterday, it's best to get to know them. While it can be almost impossible to know what is going on inside others' lives (heads), it's good to start easy. God's Holy Spirit can help us to know where to start in our sharing.

Lastly, it is important to remember that we can never "argue" someone into heaven. If things become heated, it is best to pull back. People can always sense when they, their beliefs, and their feelings are not being respected. Love has to be behind your motives and not some other kind of agenda.

So, the ball is in your court. The gauntlet is thrown down, and the challenge is laid before you. Do you think you have the guts to take your present and future into a totally new realm?

---

[1] Foster, Richard. *The Celebration Of Discipline* (New York, NY; Harper & Row, 1978) 30.

[2] Omartian, Stormie. *The Prayer That Changes Everything: The Hidden Power of Praising God* (Eugene, OR: Harvest House, 2004), 23.

Chapter 6

The Artist's Mission

The year was 1971. U.S. involvement in the Vietnam War would continue for a little less than another two years. Richard Nixon was president, and the Watergate scandal was about a year away from breaking into the headlines.

In the beginning of that year, a *Time* magazine cover story reported on the growth of the Jesus movement. It was a phenomenon that stretched to both coasts and was gaining momentum. Jesus coffee houses were popping up in almost every state. Hundreds of young folks who had previously committed themselves to the anti-establishment, "Don't trust anybody over thirty!" mindset, were turning to Jesus. He was a so-called, revolutionary, "Psychedelic Christ" for the contemporary, troubled times.

On a personal level, I was well into my junior year of high school. Posters advertising for a Christian coffee house sprung up all over the place. Having read the *Time* article, I was curious to know more about it. As I was walking home one day (something I didn't ordinarily do), a van slowed down, and I was offered a ride home. This was a more relaxed time as the threat of some dangerous, nasty, evil-minded person carting you off wasn't all that pervasive. So, I was more than glad to accept the invitation.

Inside this van was David Hanson, the driver, and a young man who I have long since forgotten. After having become nestled in the back, smiling Dave Hanson and his companion began to tell me about the coffee house that was affiliated with a nearby church. By the way, one aspect I had left out earlier in this tale was that I was walking home with my old, beaten up guitar on my back. To say that music was a gigantically important part of my life would be a horrible understatement. The previous years had been full of school choirs, bands formed by friends, and high school musicals.

Musically speaking, the Sixties and Seventies were exciting times. Since the advent of the British Rock Invasion, it was not uncommon to see kids sequestered in the empty hallways and classrooms playing their guitars. We would eagerly plop down our books in favor of picking up some new song or playing technique.

These were the socially conscious decades that gave birth to the soul-pricking, folk song movement. Anthems such as Bob Dylan's, "Blowing in the Wind," required answers to the problems facing the world. This was an all-engaging, pervasive part of my life. If you weren't into music as I was, you just weren't cool. This is one of the attitudes I carried with me as I made my trek home that day.

Dave asked me what high school I went to. When I told him that it was Spring Valley Senior High, he mentioned that some of the kids involved with the coffeehouse went to the same school. He rattled off some names, and I told him that I knew them all from classes, school choir, and the like. At some point, I mentioned that I had seen the posters for the coffeehouse in our hallways. Then came his hard sell. Not only would I be seeing kids with whom I was well acquainted, there would also be music and *cookies*! Being the original Cookie Monster, I was more than hooked.

That next Friday, I walked into the church's old sanctuary and sat down to listen to the singing. Next thing I knew, there was Jerry Mahoney, another of the many familiar school faces. His eyes widened in surprise, and his jaw dropped at least three inches when he saw me. No sooner had he seen me than he threw his arm around my shoulder, picked me up, and escorted me into another room. Something was just so totally different about the Jerry I had associated with at school. There was a "brightness" to his countenance as he walked me through the church halls. He and I always enjoyed a comfortable relationship, yet sanctuary Jerry was a 360-degree turnaround Jerry.

We entered another room, and Jerry sat me down in front of an older woman named, Mrs. Meyers. She was a kind lady who began to tell me about Jesus. Having grown up Catholic, what she said really wasn't news to me. When I relayed this fact to her, she nicely showed me John 3:16, which says,

For God so loved the world that he gave me His only begotten son. So whoever believeth in him should not perish but have everlasting life. (John 3:16, KJV)

Up until that point, my nose had never found its way into a Bible. In fact, my Catholic faith had pretty much turned it into a dusty relic, taken out of the closet only on holidays.

For the next few weeks, the coffeehouse became a weekly habit. The whole newness of the situation was a complete draw. It was not only because of the familiar company but because of the whole positively charged atmosphere. Of course, if the church had turned out to be a rather staid, gloomy, "religious" sort of situation that I had encountered in the past, I wouldn't have gone back. It was all so different and inviting.

Mrs. Meyers continued to "witness" to me (telling me about the Lord), and I really enjoyed talking to her. After a while, she made it clear that I had to accept Jesus into my heart. My first thought at that moment was I had already known about Jesus for most of my life, and I told her so. A stern look crossed her face and cut the conversation short. I knew this meant that she wouldn't be talking to me anymore, which didn't settle well with me.

A little while later, a tall, skinny guy walked into the room. Alan Walters was a talented musician with shoulder length hair who was a bit "legendary" around the church. I had heard stories about him walking up to strangers saying things like, "You should hear what the Lord did for me today." God was so alive to all of these people. He was not just some once a week, unapproachable deity who occupied the stiff, liturgy-filled services I had been accustomed to. Alan extended his hand. With a broad smile across his face, he asked, "Are you my brother?" At that moment, I knew my response couldn't be anything other than an affirmative, "Yes."

That was more than just a first step in what has turned into a more than 40-year journey with Christ. As a Catholic, I had been brought up believing that I had been born into a tradition of faith. My heavenly fate had been fixed and secured by a decision made by my grandfather's grandfather. Yet, the steps that followed that initial one in the Baptist Church proved to be something different. The "Yes" I gave Alan was a personal commitment I made to God. It was much like being married. One can go through several years together knowing your spouse and eventually begin separate lives. It really doesn't matter unless you're totally committed to each other.

The New Creature

2 Corinthians 5:17 was one of the key verses I learned when my trek began: "Therefore if any man be in Christ he is a new creature. Old things have passed away; behold all things become new." Boy, were they ever "new" for me. Not only was I associating with a lot of different people, I was learning so much.

Several years earlier, while attending my Catholic grammar school, I had learned about sin. If we were to die in our sin, our destination would be hell. The way to get rid of that sin was through confession. One big problem with sin and the pre-adolescent mind is that we really didn't know what *sin* actually was. The way I remember it, just about everything and anything we did could qualify. If we talked back to our parents, if we bothered our siblings, if we didn't eat our vegetables, if we ate too much candy... the list could've gone on forever.

In fact, as a child, I was paranoid about it all. I imagined that sin had a cumulative effect. Starting at the tippy tip of my big toe, it would be marked off until I just ran out at the tippy tip top of my head. One sin for yelling at my sister, another for not cleaning my room, and then another for leaving my underwear on the floor.

Things came to a "head" when I became tired of the "weight" that came with the belief of possibly hitting that lethal limit. So, I just gave up. Throwing caution to the wind, I decided to take my chances. After all, I had gotten to a certain point in the life and hadn't been struck down yet. I had gotten away with it all.

Even in my new life, things weren't too much better. There were some churches I attended that were against movies, television, theater, rock and roll, and various other things. Yet, being a young Christian, I took on a "soaking up" attitude. I believed just about everything I had heard. I learned to walk the walk and talk the talk. There came a point where I could proudly say, "I don't spit, cuss, smoke, or chew and I don't go with girls who do."

After some 20 years as a believer, I found that my perceived sense of perfection was impossible to sustain. In spite of the fact that I wasn't into drugs, illicit sex, or anything else largely seen as irredeemable, I saw myself as a sinner. In fact, I discovered that the bare essence of sin is not so much what we do but the intent and attitude behind it all.

What it boiled down to (just as I had picked up in grammar school) is that just about anything can qualify as *sin*. Some perceive that talking about others is "gossip" and is therefore displeasing to God. Actually, it is the intent behind the talk that makes it sin. A neighbor can speak about another neighbor very innocently, but if the speech contains inferences meant to titillate or put down others, we'd be in violation of the second of the Big Two.

The saving grace in admitting one's guilt and sinfulness is that it's a humbling release to realize that you're no better or worse than anybody else. It levels the playing field. For me, it was a tremendous weight off my shoulders because now I no longer had to keep sin at bay by what I did or didn't do. It was no longer because of my own effort. The Bible says,

> Not because of work [not the fulfillment of the Law's demands], lest any man should boast. It is not the result of what anyone can possibly do, so no one can pride himself in it or take glory to himself. (Eph. 2:9)

Now, I'm not talking about keeping or losing anybody's salvation. Anyone believing and trusting in Christ has the assurance of being with Him in paradise. The penalty of sin has been broken by Christ's death on the cross, and yet Christians are still susceptible to its effects, open to its temptation. This is especially true when we demand our own way with God.

All things are possible

Some 40 years have passed since I walked into that old sanctuary. It was that first step in a very long journey with Christ, and it has been an eventful one. There have been many times when I've lingered on the mountain tops of life and others when I've been in the dark valleys. Too many times, I've heard that the Christian life isn't hard. Others say it's "impossible." No doubt, all of us fellow journeymen (and women) have found this to be more than true as we've struggled to be more like Him.

Aha! But the good news is the admonition found in Matthew 19:26, which reminds us that nothing is impossible with God. Often, we mere mortals consider things impossible as we try to work things out on our own (as we all have a tendency to do). Take Abraham's story into consideration. God makes him an iron clad promise that the world will be blessed through him and his family, yet he consents to listen to his wife's unwise counsel in order to bring it about.

Desperately convinced that she was way beyond any feasible age for producing any sort of heir that would fulfill the Lord's prophecy, Sarai decided to count on her own way of thinking. This was her way of giving God a hand. Sarai gives her handmaid, Hagar, to Abram to sleep with and conceive a child. When the son, Ishmael, is born, things go terribly awry. What was supposed to be a very viable answer to the conception problem was a horrible mistake.

The relationship between the women soured considerably. Sarai complained to Abram that now that there was a child, things were upside down. Hagar looked upon her mistress with contempt. Undoubtedly, Abram didn't want to be bothered with the mess and told his wife to deal with it. Sarai promptly "dispatches" (beats and sends her away) Hagar and Ishmael. It was a solution to a problem that wouldn't have happened if Sarai hadn't decided to do things her own way. So much for our own efforts. The good news is we don't have to go it alone.

How joyous it is to know that He is always with us (Matt. 28:20), and it is God who started a developing and perfecting work in our lives (Phil. 1:6). Not only that, His Holy Spirit was given to lead us into all truth (John 16:13). Through the work of His presence within us, we gain the benefits of the fruit of the Holy Spirit.

Like vs. Love

Okay, let's face it. When it comes to being included in large groups of people, such as a cast for a show, we all want to be an integral part. We would all love to be liked, to get along. But it is not always very easy or simple. Actors (artists) can be notoriously "prickly." Then again, there are those who have habits that can be totally disagreeable to others.

Take what happened to me during one production as a "fer instance." During our lunch break, three of my fellow actors and I sat eating and shooting the breeze. The three relaxed, smoking cigarettes. For me, it's an awful habit, but I know that there's relatively nothing I'm going to say that's going to change their thinking on the subject. We're all adults and have heard the same AMA warnings.

One of the guys started to curse and complain about a family problem. Then, he took a bottle of rum from his pocket. Taking a swig, he passed it to the guy on his left and then to the fellow in front of him. Looking at me, he offers the bottle, and I declined. Mildly, he insisted that I just "wet my lips."

Liquor's flavors have never held any pull over my life. I've never liked the taste. And the language would have made the saltiest of sailors feel at home, but I felt I should "join in," as it were. To have run away, even in a silent huff, could have closed the doors to any future moments of being able to extend some love to them. If the situation was different and some other "intoxicants" were brought out, I would politely excuse myself, but that has never happened.

It's been the church's stance to run away from "sinners," but we three had more in common than just the show we were doing. Our common humanity knitted us together even before we met. All of us, having come from families, have to deal with family problems. Here's a point where we can all bond and empathize. We'll never be "buddy buddy" with every one we meet, but we can glory in all we have in common.

During those times when we're feeling alienated from whomever and for whatever reason, just praying and praising God for them can be a life-changing step. Praise enables us to understand how God feels about them. Unlike us, He loves them all. Keith Green wrote a great song titled, "You Put This Love in My Heart."

> There's so much more I should say if I could just find a way, You put this love in my heart. Is this real or a dream? I feel so glad I could scream, You put this love in my heart.[3]

It is so true. The love we can have toward our fellow artists is kindled by His Holy Spirit. It doesn't matter what the initial impression these people made on you was; God can change it.

In no way am I implying that reaching out to those around us is easy. Like in anything in life, you're going to find you'll be making a lot of mistakes. No doubt, the wrong words will be said here and there, but love insists that we persist. Making ourselves open and available to God will ensure that He will bring about the desired end. The important action on our part is that a viable effort is made to minister to another person.

---

[3] Keith Green. *Keith Green: The Ultimate Collection* (Milwaukee, WI: Hal Leonard), 4-5.

Resource List

There are so, so, so many books and songs out there that are available, which can aid in your (growth) walk with God. Here's a short list that could help:

Books & Other Resources

If I really believe why do I have these doubts, Lynn Anderson
When God Weeps: Why our suffering matters to the Almighty,
    Joni Eareckson Tada
Heaven: Your Real Home, Joni Eareckson Tada
The God I Love: A Lifetime of Walking with Jesus, Joni
    Eareckson Tada
The Purpose Driven Life, Rick Warren
Simply Christian: Why Christianity Makes Sense, N.T. Wright
Contemplative Prayer, Thomas Merton
Power Through Prayer, E.M. Bounds
Spiritual Direction and Meditation, Thomas Merton
The Healing Gifts of the Holy Spirit, Agnes Sanford
The Imitation of Christ, Thomas A Kempis
The Practice Of the Presence of God, Brother Lawrence
The Screwtape Letters, CS Lewis
Mere Christianity, CS Lewis
A Grief Observed, CS Lewis
Reflections on the Psalms, CS Lewis
From Prison To Praise, Merton R. Carothers
Hey God!, Frank Foglio
Walking On Water, Madeleine L'Engle
The Christian, The Arts and the Truth, Frank Gaebelin
Art and the Bible, Francis A. Shaefer
Reaching Out, Henri Nouwen

Celebration of Discipline, Richard Foster
Knowing God, J I Packer
Experiencing God, Henry T. Blackaby and Claude King
100 Plus Motivational Moments for Writers and Speakers,
   Compiled by Donna Goodrich, Mary Lou Klinger
   and Jan Potter
The Christian Imagination, Leland Ryken
State of the Arts: From Bezalel to Mapplethorpe, Gene Edward
   Veith,Jr.
God Through the Looking Glass: Glimpses from the arts,
   William David Spencer, Aida Besancon Spencer
The Prayer That Changes Everything: The Hidden Power of
   Praising God, Stormie Omartian
God Is Not Dead, Rice Broocks
The Topical Memory System, The Navigators

Music

America's 25 Favorite Praise and Worship Choruses Vols. 1-4
America's 25 Favorite Hymns Vols. 1-3
America's 25 Favorite Old Time Gospel Songs Vol.1
Songs 4 Worship:
   Shout To The Lord
   Holy Ground
   Be Glorified
   Country
   Amazing Love
   Great Is The Lord
   Give You My Heart
   My Redeemer Lives

Sing Out
En Espanol
Come and Worship
Sanctuary
Gospel
Feel the Power
In Your Presence
Prepare the way
All Things are Possible
We Exalt You
Southern Gospel
Keith Green: The Ultimate Collection
Lift Him Up, Ron Kenoly
Friends for a Lifetime, Claire Lynch

Bibliography

Foster, Richard. *The Celebration of Discipline.* New York, NY: Harper & Row, 1978.

Green, Keith. *Keith Green: The Ultimate Collection.* Milwaukee, WI.

Omartian, Stormie. *The Prayer That Changes Everything: The Hidden Power of Praising God.* Eugene, Or: Harvest House, 2004.